What Does A Police Horse Do?

Ellen F. Feld
Photographed by John Cebula

Dedicated to all the men and women in blue,
and their equine and K-9 partners,
who keep us all safe. Thank you!

I would like to thank Officer Eric Lukacs, his equine partner Liam, and all the officers of the Lancaster, PA Police Department, as well as the Bethlehem, PA Police Department for welcoming us to their cities and helping to make this book a reality. I must also thank John Cebula, who patiently set up each shot for this book with a smile on his face.

Library of Congress Catalog Card Number: 2018910525

ISBN: 978-0-9831138-9-8

Direct inquiries to: Willow Bend Publishing
P.O. Box 304
Goshen, MA 01032
www.willowbendpublishing.com

Photography by John Cebula
Book design by Creative Publishing Book Design

Printed in USA

My name is Liam. I have a very special job...

I am a police horse!

I work with a partner – his name is Officer Eric Lukacs.

There are several other horses and dogs who work with our police department.

Ozzy

Duke

Axel

Charlie

I am a police officer and have a real badge that I wear whenever I go out in public. My job is to "serve and protect" everybody who lives in our city.

A police horse has to go through any obstacle that might be found out on patrol. We learn how to do this by practicing going over all sorts of different things. We walk over tarps and water noodles...

and might even run through smoke!

One of my jobs is to go on patrol with Officer Lukacs around the city. Before I can do that, I have to take a bath. I like getting all wet!

After my bath, we head downtown
to start our patrol.

While on patrol, we meet lots of nice people. If somebody needs help, we are there to assist them.

Sometimes while on patrol, we might work with other officers such as Officer Alexander and his K-9 partner Axel.

Officer Lukacs might have to talk with another officer who may be driving around in a police car.

Sometimes we go to a local park that has a water fountain. I love playing in the water.

One of my favorite jobs is going to schools and meeting with the students. Officer Lukacs tells them what a police officer can do for them if they ever need help. I enjoy getting all the attention.

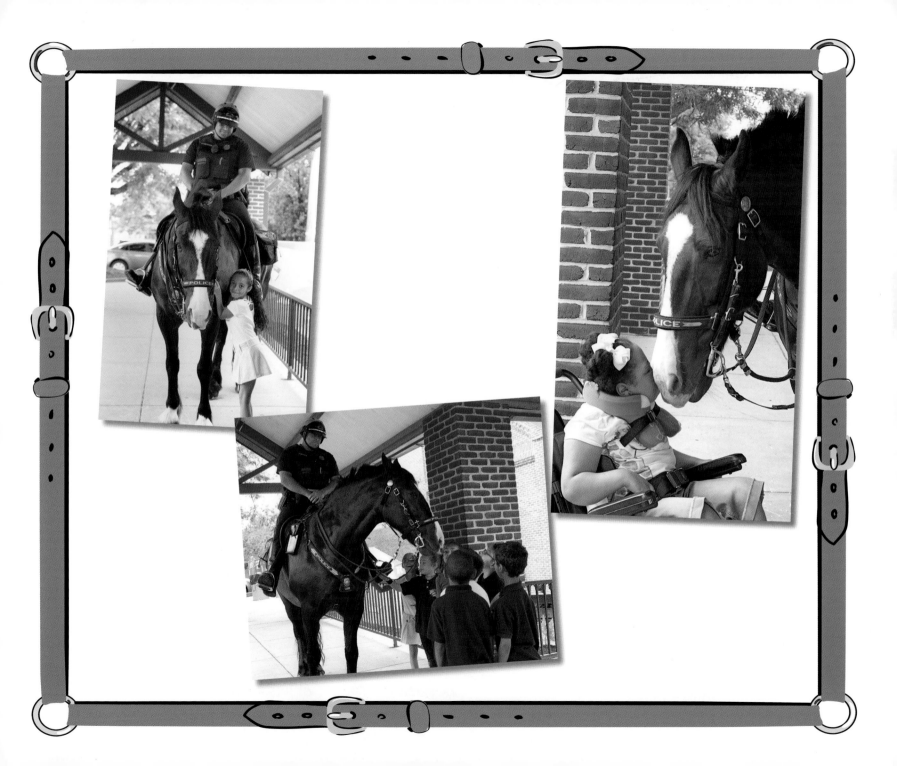

If there is a large event, like a music festival, where thousands of people come to have fun, the mounted patrol is there to keep everybody safe. At these events, we head out in groups of two to patrol.

At big events, if somebody needs help (maybe they are lost or unable to find their friends), a mounted officer, who is up high on a horse, is much easier to see than a police officer who is walking around like everybody else.

If the event is held at night, the mounted officers will be there too! We patrol day and night.

At the end of our patrol, I get to return to the barn and have some fun before starting all over again tomorrow.